A Wee Word Before We Begin...

So, ye've picked up a book full of Scottish slang, eh? Good on ye.

Whether you're a curious traveler, a homesick Scot, or just someone who heard "ya bawbag!" in a pub and needed answers – welcome. You're about to step into a world of banter, belly laughs, and brilliant expressions that make Scottish English one of the richest and rowdiest tongues on the planet.

This isn't just about translating odd words. It's about understanding the spirit behind them – the cultural swagger of Glasgow patter, the dry wit of Edinburgh sarcasm, the Doric charm of Aberdeen, and the poetic toughness of the Highlands. Every entry in this book carries a wee bit of history, character, and a whole lotta attitude.

How to Use This Book

Each page features two Scottish slang terms, presented with:

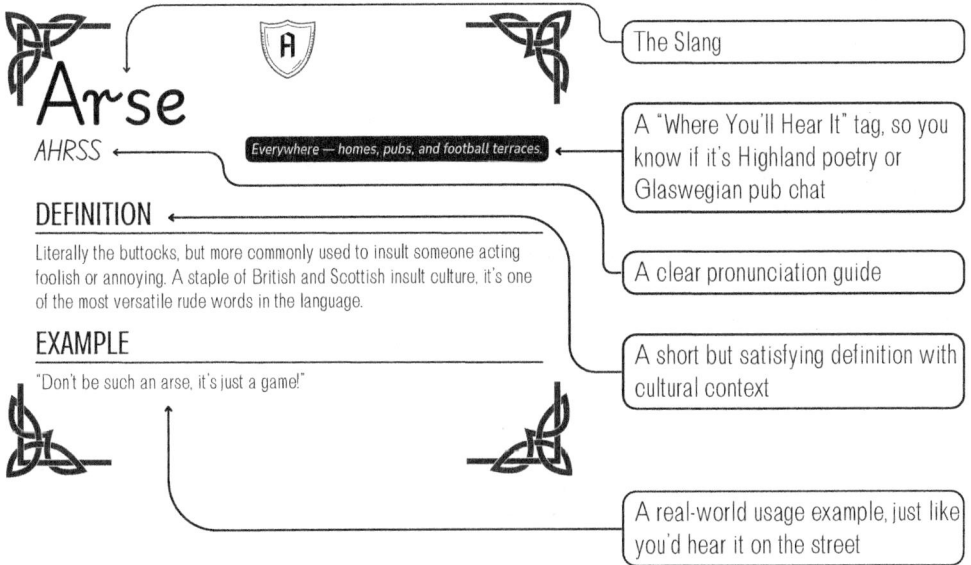

A

Arse

AHRSS

Everywhere — homes, pubs, and football terraces.

DEFINITION

Literally the buttocks, but more commonly used to insult someone acting foolish or annoying. A staple of British and Scottish insult culture, it's one of the most versatile rude words in the language.

EXAMPLE

"Don't be such an arse, it's just a game!"

The Slang

A "Where You'll Hear It" tag, so you know if it's Highland poetry or Glaswegian pub chat

A clear pronunciation guide

A short but satisfying definition with cultural context

A real-world usage example, just like you'd hear it on the street

So, take a deep breath, pour yersel a wee dram, and dive in.

This is Scottish slang — raw, ridiculous, and absolutely reekin' wi' personality.
Let's get torn in, ya dancer!

Arse

AHRSS

DEFINITION

Literally the buttocks, but more commonly used to insult someone acting foolish or annoying. A staple of British and Scottish insult culture, it's one of the most versatile rude words in the language.

EXAMPLE

"Don't be such an arse, it's just a game!"

Awrite

UH-REET

Urban Scotland — especially in Glasgow and Edinburgh.

DEFINITION

A laid-back Scottish greeting meaning 'Alright?' or 'How are you?'. It's not really a question – more like a verbal nod among pals.

EXAMPLE

"Awrite, big man?"

Aye

EYE

DEFINITION

The classic Scottish word for 'yes'. With roots in Middle English, it's still widely used in everyday speech — often stretched out or shortened depending on mood.

EXAMPLE

"Aye, I'll come by later."

Bairn

BAYRN

Common in Edinburgh, Fife, and the Lowlands.

DEFINITION

Means 'child' or 'baby', rooted in Old English and still a proud part of Scots dialect today. Used affectionately across generations.

EXAMPLE

"She's got two wee bairns runnin' aboot."

Baltic

BALL-TICK

Across Scotland, especially in winter.

DEFINITION

Used to describe freezing weather – as cold as the Baltic Sea. It's a humorous exaggeration that Scots love using even when it's just mildly chilly.

EXAMPLE

"Get yer coat, it's pure Baltic out!"

Bam

BAM

Mostly in Glasgow and surrounding schemes.

DEFINITION

Short for 'bampot' – a daft or aggressive idiot. The word's believed to originate from Glasgow and now sees wide use among youth.

EXAMPLE

"He went full bam at the bouncer."

Barry

BAH-REE

DEFINITION

Edinburgh slang for something excellent, great, or cool. Might've started as a personal name but now it's pure positivity.

EXAMPLE

"That gig was pure barry, like!"

Bawbag

BAW-BAG

DEFINITION

Literally a scrotum, but most often used as a cheeky insult for someone annoying or stupid. Famously used in a storm name – 'Hurricane Bawbag'.

EXAMPLE

"Move yersel, ya bawbag!"

Belter
BELL-TUR

DEFINITION

Can mean something amazing (a 'belter of a song')or someone who's a bit of a laugh. Derived from the idea of something hitting hard — in a good way.

EXAMPLE

"That new tune is an absolute belter!"

Bevvy
BEV-EE

In pubs and party scenes across Scotland.

DEFINITION

Alcoholic drink, especially when going out socially. Derived from 'beverage', but no one's ordering juice when they say it.

EXAMPLE

"Let's grab a wee bevvy before the game."

Blether

BLETH-UR

DEFINITION

A long, often idle, chat. To 'have a blether' is to gossip or natter, a cherished pastime in Scottish homes.

EXAMPLE

"We had a right good blether o'er tea."

Blootered

BLOO-TURD

DEFINITION

Very drunk. Comes from 'blooter', meaning to hit — as in being totally knocked out by booze.

EXAMPLE

"He was blootered after three pints."

Boggin'

BAW-GIN

DEFINITION

Something that's disgusting, dirty, or just gross. Often used to describe smells, clothes, or hygiene crimes.

EXAMPLE

"Yer socks are pure boggin'!"

Boke

BOHK

DEFINITION

To gag or vomit. Also used to describe something so nasty it makes you want to spew. Vivid, graphic, and very Scottish.

EXAMPLE

"That smell's making me boke!"

Bonnie

BON-NEE

Across all of Scotland, especially in romantic or poetic speech.

DEFINITION

Means pretty or attractive. With Gaelic roots, it's often used to describe women or scenic views — think 'Bonnie Prince Charlie'.

EXAMPLE

"Aye, she's a bonnie lass."

Braw

BRAH

Common across the Lowlands and Highlands alike.

DEFINITION

Something excellent, nice, or fine. An old Scots word that's still going strong in everyday speech.

EXAMPLE

"That's a braw jacket, pal."

Cannae

CAN-EH

Universal Scottish usage — old and young.

DEFINITION

Means 'cannot'. A Scots contraction that's used in every setting from casual chat to drama scripts.

EXAMPLE

"I cannae deal wi' this nonsense."

Chancer

CHAN-SUR

Workplaces, pubs, and family chats.

DEFINITION

Someone who pushes their luck or takes a chance, often cheekily. It can be admiration or scorn depending on tone.

EXAMPLE

"He's a chancer, asking for a raise after one week!"

Chore

CHOR

Playgrounds, housing estates, and crime stories.

DEFINITION

To steal or nick something. Often used by kids or in working-class banter.

EXAMPLE

"Somebody chored ma bike!"

Clipe

KLIP

Schoolyards and family homes.

DEFINITION

A snitch or someone who tells on others – especially in school settings. Derived from older Scots and still used widely among kids.

EXAMPLE

"Don't clipec on me to the teacher!"

Crabbit

CRAB-IT

DEFINITION

Describes someone who's grumpy, moody, or downright miserable. Often said with affection, especially when referring to an older relative in a foul mood.

EXAMPLE

"My gran's pure crabbit till she's had her tea."

Craic

CRACK

Everywhere from pubs to football matches and ceilidhs.

DEFINITION

Originally Irish, but beloved in Scotland too — means good banter, fun, or gossip. Asking 'What's the craic?' is like saying 'What's happening?'

EXAMPLE

"Come to the pub — the craic's brilliant tonight!"

Dae

DAY

DEFINITION

The Scots word for 'do'. Used constantly in speech, often in questions and commands.

EXAMPLE

"Dae ye ken whit ah mean?"

Dafty

DAFF-TEE

Among friends and families across Scotland.

DEFINITION

A harmless fool, someone acting silly or ridiculous. Not always insulting – often used playfully.

EXAMPLE

"You're a right dafty, you are!"

Dinnae

DIN-EH

DEFINITION

Means 'don't'. A core piece of Scots grammar, it turns up in nearly every casual conversation.

EXAMPLE

"Dinnae touch that, it's hot!"

Dobber

DOB-UR

Pub banter and teen slang.

DEFINITION

A crude insult for someone being an idiot or a jerk. Literally slang for a penis — but mostly used to mock someone's actions.

EXAMPLE

"Stop being a dobber and help me, will ye?"

Dreich

DREEK

DEFINITION

Perfectly captures Scotland's famously miserable weather – grey, damp, drizzly, and soul-sapping. One of the most iconic Scots words.

EXAMPLE

"It's pure dreich oot there the day."

Eejit

EE-JIT

Across the entire country — family homes and comedy shows alike.

DEFINITION

Scottish take on 'idiot', but softer and often used affectionately. Calling someone an eejit is a national pastime.

EXAMPLE

"He tried to fix the boiler with a spoon – total eejit."

Eh

AY

DEFINITION

Used at the end of a sentence to seek agreement, show surprise, or just fill a pause – much like 'right?' or 'huh?'

EXAMPLE

"That was some game, eh?"

Empty

EM-TEE

Among teens and in coming-of-age stories.

DEFINITION

A party at someone's house while their parents are out. Teenagers' favourite kind of gathering.

EXAMPLE

"You heard? There's an empty at Ryan's!"

Fanny

FAN-EE

DEFINITION

Not the American 'butt' – in the UK and Scotland, it's a crude term for female genitals. Used as a sharp insult meaning someone's being daft or pathetic.

EXAMPLE

"You absolute fanny, you dropped the pie!"

Feart

FEERT

DEFINITION

Means scared or frightened. Commonly used to mock someone for lacking courage.

EXAMPLE

"You too feart to go on the rollercoaster?"

Fud

FUHD

DEFINITION

Vulgar slang for female genitals – but often thrown around as a punchy insult for someone acting like a real idiot.

EXAMPLE

"He reversed into his own bin – what a fud!"

Gaff

GAFF

DEFINITION

A flat or house – particularly when referring to where a party's being held.

EXAMPLE

"We're heading back to Ally's gaff."

Gallus

GAL-US

Glasgow and surrounding towns.

DEFINITION

Bold, cheeky, and full of swagger. A compliment in Glasgow if you're confident without being arrogant.

EXAMPLE

"He walked in like he owned the place – gallus as ever."

Glaikit

GLAY-KIT

Family homes and classrooms alike.

DEFINITION

Describes someone with a blank, dopey, or vacant look. Can mean you're being slow on the uptake.

EXAMPLE

"Don't sit there wi' that glaikit face!"

Greet

GREET

DEFINITION

To cry or sob. A very old Scots word still going strong, especially with kids or dramatic adults.

EXAMPLE

"She was greetin' after watching that sad film."

Greet

GREET

Scottish households and playgrounds.

DEFINITION

To cry or sob. A very old Scots word still going strong, especially with kids or dramatic adults.

EXAMPLE

"She was greetin' after watching that sad film."

Gubbed

GUBD

DEFINITION

Thoroughly beaten – in a game, a fight, or even just by life. You've been absolutely gubbed.

EXAMPLE

"We got gubbed 5-0 in the final."

Gutties

GUT-EES

West of Scotland, especially schools.

DEFINITION

Old-school term for cheap gym shoes or plimsolls, mostly used in the West.

EXAMPLE

"Don't forget your gutties for PE!"

Hackit

HACK-IT

DEFINITION

Used to describe someone (often a woman)who looks rough, ugly, or worn out – usually as an insult.

EXAMPLE

"She turned up lookin' pure hackit."

Haver

HAY-VER

DEFINITION

To talk nonsense or ramble on. Immortalized in The Proclaimers' song – 'And if I haver, I know I'm gonna be, I'm gonna be the man who's havering to you.'

EXAMPLE

"He was pure haverin' about aliens again."

Hen

HEN

Glasgow, corner shops, and local cafes.

DEFINITION

A term of endearment for women — similar to 'love' or 'darling'.
Affectionate and commonly used by older Scots, especially in the West.

EXAMPLE

"Awright, hen? How's yer day?"

Hummin'

HUM-IN

All across Scotland — especially post-pub or post-football.

DEFINITION

Something that smells absolutely foul. Can also describe a person or
performance that's particularly awful.

EXAMPLE

"Your feet are hummin' after that shift."

Hunners

HUNN-ERS

DEFINITION

Means 'hundreds' or 'a lot'. Used for emphasis, often exaggerated for comic effect.

EXAMPLE

"He's got hunners of trainers, man!"

Hunners

HUNN-ERS

DEFINITION

Means 'hundreds' or 'a lot'. Used for emphasis, often exaggerated for comic effect.

EXAMPLE

"He's got hunners of trainers, man!"

Jake
JAYK

Working-class areas and cautionary tales.

DEFINITION

Short for 'jakey' – a derogatory term for an alcoholic or someone who's visibly down-and-out.

EXAMPLE

"He's turned into a total jake since losing his job."

Jobby
JAW-BEE

Homes, schools, and Scottish comedy shows.

DEFINITION

A humorous or child-friendly word for poop. An iconic and oddly beloved Scottish term.

EXAMPLE

"There's a jobby in the bath! That dug again!"

Ken

KEN

Eastern Scotland and rural areas.

DEFINITION

Means 'know'. An old Scots word still used in speech — often as a filler or tag question.

EXAMPLE

"I dinnae ken what he's on about."

Lassie

LASS-EE

Nationwide — friendly and poetic settings.

DEFINITION

A girl or young woman. The classic feminine counterpart to 'laddie'. Still a term of affection in modern use.

EXAMPLE

"That lassie's got some voice on her!"

Loon

LOON

DEFINITION

Means boy or young man in the Doric dialect of the Northeast. Also sometimes used for a daft guy elsewhere.

EXAMPLE

"He's a fine wee loon fae Aberdeen."

Mad wae it

MAD WAY IT

Clubs, festivals, and Friday nights in Scotland.

DEFINITION

Extremely drunk or out of control. Common party talk and social media phrase.

EXAMPLE

"She was mad wae it at the wedding!"

Manky

MANK-EE

Family homes and school halls.

DEFINITION

Filthy, disgusting, or generally gross. Can be used for clothes, behavior, or even weather.

EXAMPLE

"Change yer manky socks!"

Maw

MAW

Every Scottish household.

DEFINITION

Mum or mother. The Scottish take on 'mom', used with affection (and sometimes exasperation)

EXAMPLE

"Maw, where's the iron?"

Messages

MEH-SAJ-IZ

All over Scotland — especially older generations.

DEFINITION

Groceries or items picked up from the shop. If you're 'away for the messages', you're doing the food run.

EXAMPLE

"Am just away tae get the messages."

Minging

MING-IN

Among teens, TikTok rants, and hungover mornings.

DEFINITION

Something that's absolutely disgusting. A word that practically makes you gag just hearing it.

EXAMPLE

"That kebab looks minging, mate."

Mockit

MOCK-IT

Mothers shouting from laundry rooms across the nation.

DEFINITION

Very dirty or grimy – a word that almost smells. You don't want to be described as mockit.

EXAMPLE

"Those jeans are mockit – in the wash now!"

Muckle

MUH-KUL

The Borders, Highlands, and traditional storytelling.

DEFINITION

Means big or large – often used to emphasize scale. A holdover from older Scots.

EXAMPLE

"That's a muckle big spider!"

Nae bother

NAY BOH-THUR

DEFINITION

No problem. A friendly, laid-back way to say everything's cool.

EXAMPLE

"Cheers for the lift!" – "Nae bother, pal."

Naw

NAW

DEFINITION

The Scots way to say 'no'. Sharp, short, and unmissable.

EXAMPLE

"Naw, I'm no going tae that again."

Ned

NED

Urban areas, especially Glasgow and west coast.

DEFINITION

Stereotypical urban youth, often in tracksuits and up to no good. Said to mean 'Non-Educated Delinquent' – but origin debated.

EXAMPLE

"The park's full of neds on scooters."

Numpty

NUMP-TEE

Friendly teasing across all of Scotland.

DEFINITION

Lovable fool. A harmless, often funny idiot – not usually meant to be mean.

EXAMPLE

"I locked the keys in the car. What a numpty!"

Och

OCH (LIKE 'LOCH')

DEFINITION

An all-purpose Scottish exclamation expressing frustration, surprise, or resignation – like 'oh' or 'ugh'.

EXAMPLE

"Och, I've spilt it again!"

Patch

PATCH

DEFINITION

To ignore or blank someone – especially in texting or dating. Being 'patched' means being snubbed.

EXAMPLE

"She totally patched me after I asked her out."

Peely-wally

PEE-LEE-WAL-EE

Workplaces, homes, and mum-speak.

DEFINITION

Pale, sickly, or looking under the weather. Usually said with concern or mockery.

EXAMPLE

"You're lookin' awful peely-wally today."

Pelters

PELL-TERS

Football, pubs, banter-heavy workplaces.

DEFINITION

Abuse or mocking criticism – getting a roasting. If you're getting pelters, people are ripping into you.

EXAMPLE

"He got pelters for turning up late again."

Piece

PEECE

DEFINITION

A sandwich or snack, especially one packed for lunch. 'Jeely piece' = jam sandwich.

EXAMPLE

"Bring a piece for your lunch, son."

Puggled

PUG-ULD

DEFINITION

Exhausted, out of breath, or worn out — physically or mentally.

EXAMPLE

"Ah'm puggled after that walk up the hill."

Pure

PYOOR

DEFINITION

Used as an intensifier — means 'really' or 'very'. Adds emphasis in informal speech.

EXAMPLE

"That was pure mental, by the way."

Puss

PUSS

Mums, aunties, and playgrounds.

DEFINITION

Face — especially when someone's scowling or being miserable.

EXAMPLE

"Wipe that puss off yer face!"

Quine

KWINE

DEFINITION

Girl or young woman in Doric dialect. Still widely used in the northeast of Scotland.

EXAMPLE

"That quine's from Peterheid."

Radge

RAJ

DEFINITION

A crazy or aggressive person. Can also be used as a verb: 'to go radge'.

EXAMPLE

"He went radge when his team lost."

Randan

RAN-DAN

Pubs, clubs, and party recaps.

DEFINITION

A wild night out involving heavy drinking and potential mayhem. A proper Scottish bender.

EXAMPLE

"We were on the randan till 4am."

Rocket

RAW-KIT

Glasgow slang, TikTok, and comedy shows.

DEFINITION

An idiot or someone acting daft – with a bit of cheek. Not a compliment.

EXAMPLE

"He was dancing on the table – what a rocket."

Salt 'n' Sauce

SALT AN SAWSS

DEFINITION

An Edinburgh chippy classic — brown sauce mixed with vinegar instead of ketchup or salt & vinegar.

EXAMPLE

"Chips wi' salt 'n' sauce, please."

Scran

SCRAN

All over Scotland, especially among students and workers.

DEFINITION

Food or a meal — usually something hearty or satisfying. Can be a noun or a verb.

EXAMPLE

"Let's get some scran, I'm starving."

Scunnered

SKUN-ERD

Used everywhere — especially in rants or tired sighs.

DEFINITION

Fed up, sick of it, or totally done with something. A pure mood word.

EXAMPLE

"I'm scunnered wi' this rain."

Skelp

SKELP

Common in family settings or banter.

DEFINITION

To smack or slap, usually playfully – or used to describe a quick hit.

EXAMPLE

"You'll get a skelp on the lug if you don't behave."

Skint

SKINT

Universally Scottish, especially near payday.

DEFINITION

Completely broke or out of money. A regular state of being after a night out.

EXAMPLE

"Can't come out, I'm pure skint."

Sound

SOOND

Across Scotland, especially west coast.

DEFINITION

Means fine, decent, or okay. Also used to describe a reliable, good person.

EXAMPLE

"Aye, he's sound – helped me move house."

Steamin

STEE-MIN

DEFINITION

Very drunk – steaming drunk. A top-tier party state.

EXAMPLE

"She was steamin' after three gins."

Stoater

STOW-TER

DEFINITION

Something or someone amazing – could be a brilliant event, outfit, or even a person.

EXAMPLE

"That was a stoater of a match!"

Stooshie

STOO-SHEE

In the press, politics, or any family dinner row.

DEFINITION

A commotion, fuss, or minor scandal – often blown out of proportion. Adds drama to even the smallest squabble.

EXAMPLE

"There was a right stooshie over the parking space."

Swatch

SWOTCH

Common in conversations among friends or coworkers.

DEFINITION

A quick look or glance at something. Also used when asking to borrow or check something out.

EXAMPLE

"Gie's a swatch at the paper, will ye?"

Taps aff

TAPS AFF

Glasgow on sunny days, beer gardens, and memes.

DEFINITION

Means 'tops off' – a celebratory state when the sun comes out and Scots whip off their shirts. A rare but sacred occasion.

EXAMPLE

"It's 18°C – taps aff!"

Tassie

TASS-EE

Traditional households and old-school cafés.

DEFINITION

Cup or mug – especially one used for tea. A quaint and cozy word.

EXAMPLE

"Fancy a wee tassie o' tea?"

Tattie

TAT-EE

DEFINITION

Potato – the staple of every Scottish plate. Appears in dishes like 'tattie scones' and 'mince and tatties'.

EXAMPLE

"Mash the tatties for the roast, will ye?"

Tea

TEE

DEFINITION

Not just the drink – in Scotland, 'tea' often means your evening meal. Context is key!

EXAMPLE

"What's for tea the night?"

Teuchter

TYOOCH-TER

DEFINITION

A mildly insulting term for someone from the rural Highlands – used by city folk, but also reclaimed with pride.

EXAMPLE

"He's a proper teuchter, straight from the croft."

Tube

TOOB

Glasgow, football fans, and roast sessions.

DEFINITION

A fool or an idiot – not to be confused with the subway. A very Glaswegian way of calling someone daft.

EXAMPLE

"You total tube, that was the wrong turn!"

Wean

WAYNE

Glasgow and west coast family talk.

DEFINITION

Child or toddler. Short for 'wee one', it's a warm term used often by parents and grannies.

EXAMPLE

"The wean's up again at 3am!"

Weapon

WEP-IN

Slagging matches, football crowds, TikTok.

DEFINITION

Someone acting dangerously daft – not literally armed, but often out of control or embarrassing.

EXAMPLE

"He showed up in a Spider-Man onesie – total weapon."

Wee

WEE

DEFINITION

Small – perhaps the most iconic Scots word. Can be used for nearly anything: a wee dram, a wee nap, a wee job.

EXAMPLE

"Just a wee bit of milk in my tea, thanks."

Weegie

WEE-JEE

Outside Glasgow... or as self-identification with pride.

DEFINITION

Someone from Glasgow. Used by others across Scotland – sometimes lovingly, sometimes mockingly.

EXAMPLE

"The Weegies are always first on the dancefloor."

Wheesht

HWEESHT

DEFINITION

Be quiet! A command to hush, often used with children or in heated moments.

EXAMPLE

"Wheesht, I'm on the phone!"

Whitey

WHY-TEE

DEFINITION

A sudden bout of nausea or vomiting – especially after too much booze. Often comes with going pale (hence the name)

EXAMPLE

"He spewed all over the cab – pure whitey!"

Winch

WINCH

DEFINITION

To kiss or make out with someone – often a short-term, flirty thing.

EXAMPLE

"She was winchin' him behind the chippy."

Ya dancer!

YA DAN-SUR

DEFINITION

An exclamation of joy or celebration – like saying 'Yesss!' when something good happens.

EXAMPLE

"Scored in the 90th minute – ya dancer!"

Yaldy

YAL-DEE

DEFINITION

An excited cheer or shout – used when you're absolutely buzzin' about something.

EXAMPLE

"I passed ma test – yaldy!"

Yon

YON

DEFINITION

Means 'that' or 'those' – a poetic or old-fashioned way to point at something far away.

EXAMPLE

"Look at yon clouds rolling in."

Young Team

YUNG TEEM

DEFINITION

A group of teens hanging around – often associated with gangs or youth culture.

EXAMPLE

"The Young Team were oot spray painting again."

Youse

YOOZ

DEFINITION

Plural of 'you'. Used to refer to a group of people – informal but very common.

EXAMPLE

"Whit are youse daein' here?"

Printed in Dunstable, United Kingdom